BREAKING
THE VIDEO GAME
ADDICTION

ADVICE FROM A FORMER GAMER

Byron Lonewolf

WestBow
PRESS®
A DIVISION OF THOMAS NELSON
& ZONDERVAN

WestBow Press books may be ordered through booksellers or by contacting:

WestBow Press
A Division of Thomas Nelson & Zondervan
1663 Liberty Drive
Bloomington, IN 47403
www.westbowpress.com
844-714-3454

ISBN: 978-1-4908-8274-1 (sc)
ISBN: 978-1-4908-8276-5 (hc)
ISBN: 978-1-4908-8275-8 (e)

Library of Congress Control Number: 2015908878

Print information available on the last page.

WestBow Press rev. date: 01/05/2024

Contents

Preface

One night, I had awoken to an unexpected and bizarre experience. Strange and twisted images appeared in my mind. They were images and sensations that religious people and others would call "hell". It was a place that had flames, torment and suffering. In the background there were various demons, one resembling the emperor from *Star Wars*, another like *Jaba the Hut* that appeared to laugh at my situation, characters that seemed to come from *Hell Raiser*; from the very games and movies that we partake.

I looked up to see a dark spirit, and a man like Moses standing beside him with Jesus at his side. It was weird. Jesus was small. Then I heard a voice screaming and holding a bible saying do you believe in Jesus. Like a fool, not aware of what was going on, I said its religion and Jesus that is the reason all of this was happening. I felt Jesus was sad. And I heard laughter. The laughter of women, probably the soul ties.

I thought it was just a strange dream and wanted to go back to sleep. Then I recall falling into a pit with brown clouds around me. I called out and saw a plane shaped like a white dove hovering above me. I called out again and I saw Jesus. I saw him from a distance and there were these glass walls between us. I could not bring him into my heart. It was sad.

When I failed to reach Jesus, and realizing that my relationship with him was pathetic to say the least, I found myself falling into a pit. That white craft resembling a dove was hovering above it. I called out, then moments later a flickering flame appeared above my head and something (which I believe to be my serotonin) was sucked from my brain. The sad part was that I just wanted to go back to sleep. I didn't care. I wanted what was removed but it was gone. If it had been a visit from God, I was found to be most disrespectful. And even to this day I feel dumbfounded and see it as surreal.

The sad part was that I seemed to tolerate these entities for a short time then woke from my sleep. I seemed to have the ridiculous bravado that I wasn't bothered by such images since I had seen worse in video games and movies and had become accustomed to such images. I even recalled telling myself that it was nothing, and that I had seen worse in video games. Then all of a sudden my vision started flickering then went dark. I shot up wondering what was going on. It was this experience that brought me to the realization that Hell is a real dimension that has a great influence on our lives. Hell and Heaven, and any beliefs about a life after death may be as absurd as science fiction to the mainstream, yet I have experienced a complete distortion to my mindset, powerful enough to derail and ruin my life.

Finally this book is not an attempt to challenge your belief system, but only to warn you of something that I suspect; to wake you up. There is a hidden danger in media and in video gaming. It is a weapon of mass distraction and a means of corrupting the youth of today. I would even go as far as to say that there is a demonic agenda; and sadly games may be a doorway or a road into that realm; especially for unsuspecting children.

PART ONE –

SOME GAMES AREN'T FOR KIDS

CHAPTER ONE

A quick overview of gaming

Gaming refers to the culture of playing video games. It's about people playing their favorite games with friends at home or across the Internet. It often refers to playing games as a hobby and playing frequently. Often when someone is gaming, they are referring to playing on a home gaming console or PC computer for more than an hour a week. Also gaming may take place on computers, such as when people are playing role -playing games like *World of Warcraft* or *Guildwars*.

A **gamer** is someone who plays games more than at just a moderate level. It is a lifestyle to them. They play every day, and play a variety of games. They are familiar with the various games out there and the different platforms. A gamer also plays games beyond a moderate level. They may play on line with friends or solo at home in single player games. In many cases, a gamers' main focus is playing video games above everything else.

Consoles

A **game console**, or gaming machine, usually consists of a main unit with a CD tray and several ports for connecting controllers. The controllers are the parts of the machine held by the player that consist of buttons that direct game play. The CD tray on the main unit is where the games are inserted. The other wires on the machine connect to the television set and a power source. Consoles are generally simple to set up and simple to operate.

There are tons of game output devices out there ranging from consoles in a living room to a cell phone. The three main consoles (game machines) in the home currently as of this writing are the **Xbox 360 and now Xbox 1**, the **Nintendo WII and WII U**, and the **PlayStation 3 and now 4**. I express that these are the systems as of the time of this writing because the technology is constantly improving and new products are constantly emerging. So little emphasis will be about the systems and more about games.

These platforms will be the main focus in this book since they are the preferred consoles by choice for children ranging from 3 to 15. People ages 16 to adulthood will mainly use these consoles too in addition to computers, cell phones and iPads in order to meet their gaming needs. However my focus here is on the child and not so much the adult; although adults may definitely benefit from what is mentioned in this book especially the later chapters.

Xbox series 10

The Xbox 360 is the console I have played on for some time and is the sequel to the Xbox. The Xbox One is new at the time of this writing so I will mainly focus on the XBOX 360 here. Popular games such as HALO have kept me loyal to the system. In addition, this being the system of choice among friends, has kept me attached to that console as opposed to the others. I like it because of the simple interface, the games, and the xbox live features.

Xbox live is the online feature of the system that allows for the player to play friends online at any hour and create a buddy list. I am able to play and talk with my friends, view their online profile and avatar, compare game achievements and leave messages with them. In fact often times, I would simply leave a message for them via Xbox live instead of calling them because I knew they would log into their account on a regular basis.

The Nintendo Switch

The Nintendo WII is a gaming console popular among families' with children. Parents like it because of the large choice of kid friendly games and the types of games that allow for multiple players. The controllers and system are designed to allow the child to move around and interact allowing a high degree of motor activity compared to the other systems. They are fun and provide a good degree of motor movement.

The PlayStation 5

The PlayStation 3 is the third console of the family consoles and is made by Sony. It has a large variety of video games and a blue ray player built in. The graphics on this machine are sharp. For that reason it is a little more expensive than the other system. It is similar to the Xbox in that it also has its set of controllers and disk tray.

Millions of the consoles listed above have been sold in this country and in countries across the globe. Just about every country that has an outlet probably has at least a good portion of their kids and maybe some adults playing video games. And as the older systems become more affordable, they become more available even in underdeveloped countries. And this doesn't even include the sales in computers, and other mediums for gaming.

Other gaming venues

Computers

Computers are seen as another gaming device in the home. Often gamers, especially older gamers, will play on the computer because of enhanced features that PCs offer. Graphics are better, gaming speed is better, and there are tons of games for the PC. In fact computers, like laptops or the iPad are often used because of the versatility they offer. For example, a mother at a gymnastics class sat near me playing a simple game that kept her mind occupied; which leads me to realize that people in all walks of life are embracing the gaming culture.

Many Massive Role playing games are played across the world on computers. A game like World of War craft can have multiple users playing in a game with other players from all over the world. Players build a character, level up the character, join guilds, and play against other players. These kinds of games can consume much of one's time and can also become addicting.

In addition to playing my Xbox, I have also spent a good amount of time on my laptop playing such games as *Diablo*, *StarCraft*, *Age of Empires*, *Guildwars*, and *Balders Gate*. I would play online or independently. The games on computers can be just as violent or if not more violent than those of console games. The plus side though is that there are a lot of educational software games that can be played on the home computer. There are also web sites with free games. But be vigilant because some of these games can be offensive and have hidden costs such as the ability to purchase in-game items or virtual dollars.

Handhelds & Smart Phones

Nintendo DS, PSP and other handhelds are small game devices that can be held in the palm of your hand. The types of games can vary from simple E rated games, games rated for everyone, to Harsh M rated games, games rated for mature players 18 and older. Just because it is a smaller screen, does not make the system harmless. The other possible problem is that because they are portable and are often taken out of the home, game time is extended. In addition to this they can be just as addicting to play on as the consoles.

Phones like the iphone have a multitude of game applications. While many applications may be functional and serve some purpose, many are still games. In fact many people find themselves addicted to some of the games they purchase without realizing the amount of time they spend on them. Currently two games I can think of that have become popular on cell phones are angry birds and plants vs. zombies. And there are plenty more game applications, maybe a thousand, especially with the ease of making them.

Arcades

Arcade machines in video game arcades are a familiar venue for children to play. There are games that allow them to physically interact, like dance revolution, and there are race-car games. There are also the traditional fighting games and first person shooters. And there are the table hockey tables, and ticket dispensing machines. The advantage is that these interactive games require money and so there really isn't a problem with kids spending much time on them as opposed to consoles in the home. Another vantage is that it could be a family experience. They can visit the arcade and enjoy themselves without the dangers associated with forming a lifestyle of gaming.

But still beware. Although the game is not being played at home, sinister content may now be accessible to your child since no one monitors who plays it. So a child can walk up and slip in a few tokens for what would probably be an M rated game or simply inappropriate. As I passed by one machine, some zombie slayer game, I had noticed an upside-down pentagram on the start buttons. I thought it was weird that they would have that kind of set up. Some of the other games like *house of dead* basically have you shooting zombies and other undead creatures, so be vigilant in arcades too.

Games

Games are the heart of it all. Every console is designed to play games. And games are specifically designed to entertain. Games are in the format of cartridges, disks, or downloads and are usually purchased at outlets such as Game Stop, Target, Walmart, or online such as on the console marketplace.

Video games that existed in the past were like pong, harmless and leaving much to the imagination. If it was some kind of battle, then it was between two hardly recognizable pixels that nearly resembled squares. And there was usually no blood. Even early role-playing games were mostly text with few images, some didn't even move. So the graphic details were lacking, and anything sinister or any attempt at realism was missing.

In fact I recall other games in the 70s like Asteroids and Pac man. Those games, especially with the lack of graphics and highly visual content seemed innocent in comparison to games today. They had their danger of addiction, but they didn't have the toxic and graphic content that games today have. Most of them were also in arcades instead of living rooms, and they lacked the addictive appeal that games today have. In fact today we have consoles in our homes with large plasma television sets and surround sound so that we have our own arcade. And most gamers or owners of game consoles have a small to extensive library of games.

Like the systems that games can be played on, games can be just as diverse. Games can be for a console, a computer, or a handheld device. Games can be geared for children, teens, or adults. They can be purchased used or new. They can be cheap or expensive. And games can be sublime in quality or poor in quality. Games can also have a high or low fun factor. Games can be short or long and have a replay value; which means the player can go back and play the game over again and again.

Like books and movies games are also categorized into genres. The Genres of games include: first person shooter, action, action adventure, adventure, miscellaneous, role-playing, sports, simulation, family, and strategy. Local game stores and gaming websites can break down each category and provide a more detailed description of each.

Today, the industry's goal is to make games seem as if you are really there. And that's also the experience that gamers want. The industry wants blood splattering in the air and across walls. They want gore such as arms flying off, heads exploding from bullet wounds, and as much realism as possible. Just sitting down watching a few minutes of *Call of Duty Black Ops* or playing the game *World at War* demonstrated that. In World at War, I truly felt like I was an American Soldier fighting the Japanese on some beach. Everything felt so real with the yells of fallen soldiers to the soldiers hidden in palm trees shooting bullets that whizzed by. Even the explosions that surrounded me seemed lifelike. I'm sure it would have given any veteran watching the chills or shakes.

Most vendors will ask for I.D. or ask for a parent to make the purchase of an M rated game. It is illegal to sell an M rated game to a child without the consent of a parent. Sadly though, I have heard about M rated games being purchased for children as young as eight. Parents purchase these games because of their ignorance of the ratings and content. More of this is mentioned later in the book under the tips for parents' chapter.

CHAPTER TWO

Why I believe gaming isn't for kids

Basically I think it's a gateway to hell for kids. Throw the game system out!!! The reason I feel this way is because more and more kids are playing less kid friendly games like *Sonic the hedgehog,* but are instead playing more games like *Call of Duty, Dead Space* or *Gears of War.*

Children's brains are still in a state of development. Putting this kind of information in front of them is probably worse than hours of television. That's because now they are active participants in the acts they commit instead of just watching them like innocent bystanders. And we are talking now about hours of play, on a daily basis, crossing over at times into the games they shouldn't play. And often times this happens because a game system, like a television set, is seen like a second baby sitter. So kids, generally having less self-control then adults and being left unattended, will choose to play instead of read, or watch hours of television instead of ride a bike.

For example a game like fable, meant for a more mature audience, allows the player to sleep with wenches at brothels and make human sacrifices. While that might be ok for an older teenager or adult that knows its entertainment and with a brain that is more developed, it might not be good for a ten year old. You certainly don't want to desensitize the child or make it seem as though such acts are acceptable in their young and impressionable minds. And studies are still being done to see what kind of effects these images can have on a child. And even if they don't act it out, we don't know if their internal state is a mess and if problems that arise later can be linked to it. More and more studies coming out are supporting that negative development of the brain and behaviors are occurring.

A main concern, and why I say that gaming can be a way into hell for a child, is because of what I mentioned in the preface. Do games create a lust for violence, and things demonic? Does it lower one's "vibration" or fill them with negative energy? Does it "Darken the soul?"

Again I say the experience I had and the demons I had seen weren't just nightmares or hallucinations. I wish I could call them what Atheists describe as just "invisible friends", figments of my imagination, but there is just too much that happened. My whole life has changed because of this nightmarish experience. Even after this occurred I could not go back to gaming and doing some of the other things I enjoyed without tension, without torment, without an altered state of mind. And I'm trying to prevent this from happening to you and your family, especially your innocent and unsuspecting children, Christian and non-Christian alike.

And I wonder what's going on when my teen-age son mentioned that he would like to enjoy it all and doesn't care about hell. This occurred after the incident mentioned in the preface, amidst what I reluctantly call spiritual warfare. I was shocked. I'm sure it wasn't him talking but perhaps something else, a spirit maybe. How many kids out there think the same thing? I bet most would choose playing black ops then going to church or making better choices. I guess the material world is just too inviting and seductive to this generation. It's up to us as parents to enforce or at least encourage their walk with Jesus Christ and God. It's like eating junk food all of the time over vegetables, it's like allowing your child to turn their free time into a vice over a healthy hobby.

The content in some of these games can also lead your child into a fascination with monsters and demons. In fantasy role-playing games and action adventure games we look forward to the monster boss battles and the hordes of creatures that are to be defeated. For example, zombies and vampires are dark things; and yet kids are associating with them via cartoons, games, movies, or toys.

Kids are continuing to identify with or gravitate toward dark heroes or villains, especially since the media glorifies it. The enemy out there wants us to rationalize it by saying, "Ohh *Hell Boy* is a good guy. *Darth maul* is cool! Let me be like them." We don't realize that we are becoming like them, by loosing empathy, by embracing the dark side. Soon our minds let more of that darkness in and with it the influence of sin and hate toward good things.

I first found myself fascinated with dinosaurs as a child, which isn't a problem. Then later I fell in love with fantasy and *Dungeons and Dragons*, a past time that many would think little about. So when fantasy games came out involving many of the creatures and elements of *D&D*, I found myself quickly gravitating toward them.

I would play fantasy role playing games on my PC, and my Xbox. I couldn't get enough of it. I found myself also reading fantasy when I wasn't playing the games and also watching movies with the same content. Soon I found myself gravitating toward fantasy figures on a huge almost obsessive scale. Eventually I began to collect figures, things that seem like they would be straight out of hell, and that's when it became a problem. And if that wasn't enough, I began collecting Halloween decorations, like large gargoyles and skulls, and surrounding myself with them. It was as if the darkness slowly crept in, and little known to me, it created a negative energy field that my wife could detect, strong enough for her to make a comment and to loose the desire to linger.

All that stuff, much of it dark in nature, was so contrary to the bible and a Christian life, definitely the stuff they warn you about; whether you're a believer or not. And yet I was surrounding myself with it, unaware of the negative energy they gave off, and not realizing that my thinking and discernment were becoming corrupted as I rationalized and defended the right to keep it all.

For example, the *Balrog* from *Lord of the Rings* is cool, but having a twelve-inch statue of it by your bedside would seem like you're in league with Satan. It's not healthy spiritually. It's a demon! And I had display cases filled with such stuff. I was obtuse to it.

Later, after my strange overnight experience, I destroyed and threw them out. I didn't even care that some of the figures had taken me hours to paint or cost me lots of money. I wanted to be disconnected from it. And I kid you not, strangely, upon disposing of them, including the larger figures, I felt a strange shift in my body. I felt a force tug on my body. It may have been supernatural, not sure. But I know it was the right thing to do.

The separation from such toys also made me realize I hadn't grown up. I was not living my life as my peers of my age who wouldn't have had such things surrounding them were. I can't believe how much I had been in darkness.

So if you find your child collecting toy figures like the ones mentioned above, cleanse your home of them and avoid spiritual darkness. Comic book and movie characters like *Hell Boy* and the Devil from the movie *LEGEND*, should remind you that he is the devil. I found myself liking the prince of darkness character in that movie so much that I purchased the movie and watched it many times. I even purchased the toy figure from the *Spawn* figures line. The devil is not some cuddly puppy, certainly not a character to idolize or admire. Why would you want to fellowship with a dark energy that wants to eat you and destroy your world?

So, monitor their games, their toys, and their movies and set ground rules and boundaries from the beginning and stick to them. Hell is real. It's another dimension. It's the place that's probably seen when a person roles their eyes back after their last breath, the stuff that people tell you about when having a negative near death experience. It is an energy made up of dangerous entities that cause a person to suddenly do some unspeakable act. If the enemy can get an inch, it won't be long before it takes a mile. And as the saying goes, he comes like a thief in the night to kill, steal and destroy.

My final advice for parents is, "Keep that Trojan horse out of your house!!!" Take the gaming system out unless you intend to strictly enforce it. E rated games only. I thought I could regulate it. It's hard. You don't need the added stressor in your life, family or marriage, especially when so many other things bombard us.

And if they already have it, and are in the thralls of being hooked, you may have to accidentally sabotage it. I'm not necessarily advocating this route, but if a compromise can't be reached, you might want to see a store technician on how to sabotage it without completely ruining it. In this way, it'll appear to be an accident, and the delay may give you time and options to redirect them toward a healthier hobby or lifestyle change. You might say, "whoops…looks like it's broken…I guess we'll have to fix it…later." Well let's go see a movie then. Then substitute the system with the things you want your child doing in the mean time to fill the void.

This covert route is an extreme route though, even though it avoids direct conflict, since it involves money and possibly permanent damage. It's better to be firm and upfront and pin the removal of it on poor grades, excessive play or weight gain. Then you can have a serious discussion, lay down your ground rules before returning it to them. You can also have that talk about the content of the games, and how you feel about it.

But if you still decide to get your child a game system after reading the information above then please follow the advice in the next chapter.

CHAPTER THREE

Tips for parents

Here are some tips and important information to know in order to help manage your child's game play and some precautions or measures you can take to keep gaming from interfering with your child's non-gaming life and development.

Tip 1 - Check the rating system

Pay attention to the game's rating and understand the rating system. The ratings on the game case are there to protect your child and advise you. So use them. And remember that game stores only have to comply with the law and will sell to a child if a parent is purchasing the game.

When I asked the employee at Game Stop about the age of kids that parents buy the game *Call of Duty* 4 he said, "Parents come in to buy kids as young as 8 this game." The game has an M rating which means you must be at least 18 to play.

This is very important because many titles with harmful and graphic content are sold to parents who just wanted to please their child. Don't give in!

Like many other things, games can also be purchased online without the consent of an adult. They can also be borrowed from friends. So be careful.

Tip 2 - Investigate Games Further

Websites

For more information in exploring game systems and games go to websites like **gamefaqs.com**, or **commonsensemedia. org**. Gamefaqs.com will have information about a variety of games from a variety of platforms. It is user friendly, has a description of each game, its ESRB rating, its rating regarding performance and quality (more about this below), and other helpful content. Commonsensemedia.org will have lots of information about games including their own rating system and feedback about games. They serve as a guardian angel and advocate for the family against inappropriate forms of media. In addition they offer other helpful tips in the realm of parenting too.

Game Review Shows

Game coverage shows or Game channels such as G4 on Cable will also run previews of new releases and show video game content. A show called XPLAY hosted by Adam Sessler and Morgan Webb on G4tv is a good place to get feedback. Such shows will give a critique and a visual run through of the game so that gamers will be informed.

The video game clips will give you a glimpse into the game and will help you determine if the game is appropriate. G4tv may or may not be available on your local cable network; however you may have similar channels or shows. I do believe it is available online through Netflix. This channel and the shows on it will also give you exposure to the gaming culture.

Stores

Game stores like GameStop are a good place to purchase a video game and inquire about it since the employees are highly knowledgeable and often play the games themselves. Employees should already be trained to avoid selling M rating games to children under the appropriate age and should be able to determine from their perspective if the game is appropriate for your child. However be specific in what you want and don't want in a game so that they can help you avoid the purchase of an inappropriate game. Toys R us, Target and Wallmart also have their own video game and electronic media departments with knowledgeable personnel. All of these stores usually have game kiosks or game demos set up for the public to sample. In fact most of the time you visit you will find a child playing the featured game while others watch in the background.

Magazines

Magazines like *Game Informer, PC gamer,* and *Inside Xbox* provide information on new games, consoles and accessories. They may also provide information regarding industry news and issues involving the world of gaming. The advertisements for new release games will have artwork and images to reveal the content of the game. The magazines also feature evaluations of the game to be released as well as their rating in regards to quality.

A ten is a high mark, and few games earn that rating. Most fall between 6 and 9. Games of poor quality will generally score below a five on a rating scale to ten or a 1 on a rating scale from 1 to 5. Those games are generally regarded as not playable due to visual quality and graphics, poor controls, and a poorly flushed out story with lousy characters. Games are often given ratings by the same people, whether they are for children or adults, so there may be some bias. However, I have generally found them to be fair when rating games for kids.

Youtube

YouTube is a great place to check out video game content. Many people will post actual real time video game clips as a walk through. All you need to do is type in the game title and you will see several samples or clips featuring actual game play. You can watch the player lead you through parts of the game and determine if the game is appropriate or not for your child. In addition those clips will help your child solve difficult parts of a game reducing his or her time playing and restarting over again.

Tip 3 - Watch for dark and evil content

As mentioned earlier in this book, it's proposed that things vibrate and give off a negative or positive vibration or energy.

It seems that there are also dark forces out there that aim to lead us into our own destruction, whether they are internal, external or both. And often, if we are not aware of how we, and our children, are living in the present, we can be lead into worse behaviors and become lost.

Not wanting to repeat myself here, but as mentioned above, the content in most M rated or even T rated games is harmful, especially if your child is exposed to it for hours. And playing a game imprints those images on their minds in the form of memories quite possibly for the rest of their life.

Also be vigilant of the toys they collect that are related to video games, especially the evil characters. Ask your self if they are dark or demonic. If so get rid of them. Don't even rationalize it or compromise about it. Toss it out! If it's a teenage son, express your feelings about them, and get a mediator if you have to.

So my final advice on this is to really check the ratings and the content to avoid games with such images. If you're not sure ask the vendor or do some research. Sometimes watching them play will also give you an idea of how much negative content might be on it.

Tip 4 - Help them redirect their aggression into a positive outlet

Studies have shown that video games can increase aggression; desensitize children to violence and lower feelings of sympathy. Some studies will even go as far as to say that the images and actions they perform in the game desensitizes them and lowers their ability to feel empathy toward others. Even if it's just a video game, killing, and killing, and more killing can't be good. I would think that it eventually leads toward an inward love for violence.

I once worked in a kindergarten classroom as a paraprofessional, and a child put a Lego gun to my head while I was assisting another child with reading an alphabet book. I was shocked and thought he had to learn this from somewhere.

Kids might not be acting it out on the outside, (although the above incident could be an example of it) but its possible their thinking about it on the inside.

I've often overheard conversations while with my younger son at the park and listened in on kids bragging about how they killed the enemy in Gears of War. And the kids were between 8 and 10, not even old enough to be playing that game which has an M rating.

So as mentioned above, I highly encourage that you discourage young children from playing T and M rated games. E rated only. And give lots of hugs and make them exercise. Can't hurt right?

Tip 5 - Spend time with your kids

This seems like simple advice and it's probably a cure all for everything. Yet so often we take time with our kids for granted. We're often too busy or preoccupied. But even five minutes with them and a frequent hug can do wonders. Love them and do things with them as a family so that they're not always tied up with their games. Give them a hug frequently.

Basically don't let their game system be their baby sitter. Don't allow your child to be so consumed in games that you loose out on developing a relationship with them. Ask them how their day is. A parent shouldn't simply have a relationship where they stick their head in their child's room for a five minute greeting everyday of the week. Because before you know it, your child is in high school, then college. Form those pleasant memories now.

It's important for the family to be close with each other. Family outings should be common. I try to make a habit of road trips at least twice a month. I often try to set up camping trips and weekend hikes or excursions.

See the list that I have later in this book for tips to avoid conflict with your spouse or partner. It offers a tip for the gaming spouse to watch the kids to give the other (non gaming) spouse a break. Places to take your kids are mentioned, however it's just a starting point. I'm sure you could be more elaborate and creative especially since you know your child's interests best.

Encourage them to get involved in a family activity, like doing a scrapbook together, or a family sport like volley ball. Doing things like this, might also serve to resolve any issues or tension with other members of the family.

And don't let them fight you on this. If they're already hooked on playing for long periods, start with a few minutes, taking baby steps, then build up from there.

Tip 6 - Reduce their game playtime

While watching an episode of National Geographic I learned that there is a rehab facility for video game addicts in South Korea. Apparently in South Korea they are finding so many kids becoming addicted to games, (and the same is most likely becoming true here in the USA) and the internet that they are offering support groups that focus on treating obsessions to game.

In moderation playing E rated games may be fine. But much of the time an hour turns into five hours, and before you know it, a good portion of the day that has passed has been devoted to being in front of a television screen in play. Aside from time devoted for sleep and school (or work) there is only so much more time left in the day. And remember the saying that what we spend our time doing most is eventually what we become good at. So try to make them spend more time in developing their talents in a field that will employ them in the future instead.

Games can be so time consuming that they lead your child away from important things such as school, and the improvement of talents or social skills when played excessively. Other things gaming can lead a child from could be prayer, meditation and religious studies. So make sure they know those things like schoolwork and the other things mentioned above are more important and should be done first before gaming.

Excessive gaming can also lead children away from chores and things that teach them responsibility. Continued play can distract them from things that instill a sense of value, away from godly aspects like caring for others and things that instill inner joy such as engaging in quality family time.

So limit their time on their gaming systems. Make sure they're spending more time studying, doing homework, and getting involved in educational activities. Their teachers will love you for it. And make sure they do their chores first.

Make sure they make time and don't neglect opportunities to develop talents or skills in areas such as art, music, dancing or anything that they have started an interest in that could later lead to a career or life pursuit or a life long hobby.

Encourage them to join a club or organization like the Boy Scouts of America, or the Young Marines. I'm sure there are other organizations out there, especially now that child obesity has become a problem.

Also when managing their playtime, be aware that they might be trying to clear a level when playing. Let them know in advance not to start a new attempt or game when you want them to get off soon. Make sure that they begin finding their next save or check point. Place a timer near the television set if you need to. And make sure your child knows how to save his or her game. My younger son played for three hours and got to level 6 using Yoda to fight Count Duku. Because he didn't save he had to start from the very beginning just to get back to that battle.

And if they're playing online, tell them not to begin a new session. This winding down time will give them time to move toward their goal without having to start all over again. Trust me, just shutting it off will upset anyone, especially after trying hard to complete something that required many tries.

And don't let them tell you that they will after they finish killing some boss (big monster or opponent) character. That can take hours. Just tell them they are allowed so many more tries or so many more minutes.

Tip 7 - Make sure they do their schoolwork

I really want to stress this. I know I mentioned it above in reducing their game play. But it really needs more coverage since I see the changes in education as a teacher. I have seen the efforts or lack of effort from students, observing their lack of enthusiasm for their course work and academic achievement. Yet if you ask them if they play video games, most will raise up their hand. And if you ask them how long they play, they will admit to playing for hours. And I'm finding that its not just boys; girls are also getting into gaming as well.

As I recall, nearly half the 8th grade class of my school, did not culminate in June of 2011. A large portion was excused from the graduation ceremony due to poor grades. And it seems to have gotten worse since then, with kids sneaking in their handheld electronics or phones to play instead of listening to a teaching lesson or lecture.

At a meeting about SDAI strategies (Teaching strategies to reach students at risk of failing and English Language learners), regarding testing, and preparation for the CST (California Standard Test) the main speaker had mentioned that she had trouble competing with her students against games like *Call of Duty Black Ops*. She went on to say that she learned some of the kids were spending up to eight hours a day leaving out time for their studies. And their performance is lacking because of it to say the least. She concluded that CST scores are dropping because of *Call of Duty Black Ops* and the gaming culture. In her words, "We are competing against it."

What's happening to the youth of our nation? Grades are falling, and test scores are dropping. The consequences are that kids who do become addicted or spend too much time gaming will see a drop in their schoolwork eventually. They will produce less work and work of poorer quality. Their level of understanding will become compromised. Their frustration will grow, and they'll drop out. And when they decide to pursue a higher level of education, they may not be prepared for it.

Our kids will one day be the pillars of our civilization. I want to make sure that they are just as intelligent as the generations before them when this country was great and the pursuit of learning and building was paramount.

So tutor your kids if you can. There are many workbooks and books out there that you can buy and that will help your child. I also suggest showing them Health related videos that discuss society's concerns, such as Aids, prostitution and drugs; especially now since it seems so many schools are cutting out programs as a result of budget cuts.

Remember, teachers want your child to succeed in school. I would even give some classroom workbooks out to parents during parent conference night that wanted to see an improvement in their child's grades. So ask your child's teacher for some. You can also encourage your child to read for at least 20 minutes a day, and ask them to watch educational programming.

Tip 8 - Monitor their online play

If your child is playing online, monitor it. Watch out for trash talk and Profanity! If your child were under 15 years old, I would band them from playing online unless it's a more suitable game that is geared for other kids their age. Otherwise try to mute the settings. Also be aware that they don't receive negative influence from friends on line encouraging them to play longer hours or the wrong kinds of games, and to ignore your advice.

I have observed my son's chat on several occasions and have noticed that the topic is mostly about the game. He may discuss strategies, or a past failed maneuver. He may also discuss the quality of the game he is playing or another game or game demo that he has tried. Other discussions may be about the weapons in the game or the armor. Cheats or game glitches may be discussed. I have even heard him and another player make a remark when I told my son to clean his room. The other player told my son, "Yah, you heard him." I laughed, thankful that it wasn't a jeer at me but that he was backing me up instead. Generally I found the conversation to be game related and without offense.

Most of the people on my son's buddy list were between 10 and 30, basically some younger and some older. Some of the friends on his buddy list were friends, classmates, and random players they've never met but encountered each other in matches in the past. And remember some of these "buddies" are far away. Some aren't even in the same country.

They were chosen for their talent, performance, or ability since no gamer wants a leach (Someone who does nothing but tags along and collects the loot) or a noob (a new and unskilled player). Most played *Call of Duty*. And I wasn't worried about the possibility of pedophiles since everyone in the forum is there to do one thing, "Game". That is the culture. And unless your child includes a player on their friend's list, the game venue is always changing, with new players entering to play each time.

There also seems to be a lot of policing among players. They will kick a player off if need be and report a player who is in violation of set rules or good conduct. And sometimes, sadly, it was the younger crowd that was "kicking but". So they were always welcome on a team, especially for bragging rights when challenging your other friends. But never the less, you should still be aware.

Remind your child of how their conduct should be. Remind them that when they play they should avoid the use of profanity and bullying tactics. I have had to remind my son several times not to get carried away in games by yelling out or using profanity. Basically just tell him or her to tone it down.

Tip 9 - Make sure they get their exercise in

It seems to be all over the news that more and more kids are suffering from obesity. It's from a combination of poor diet and a sedentary lifestyle. This is very bad because the end result is poor health and a shorter life span. There are also reports that the lack of activity may impair brain development that may lead to lower test scores, grades and cognitive skills.

We are a different generation than our parents and grandparents. Back then kids played together and they played outside. They could run to their neighbor's home without their parents being in fear, and were creative with their time. They build clubhouses, collected frogs, and explored their environment. They would play games like, hide n seek, tag, and Marco Polo. They were more active, they swam, they ran, they played jump rope, football, baseball and soccer at a nearby park or on their lawns. They read more and seemed to be more focused on their athletic abilities and academic achievements.

Now kids are less active, watching television or gaming, especially for hours. And this can cause additional health problems besides obesity. Vision problems can occur, wrist or carpal tunnel syndrome can happen with keyboards used for computer games, and the problems associated from poor sleep habits due to all night gaming. The obesity, itself, can lead to poor heart health and diabetes.

To reduce these harmful consequences related to gaming, enrich their life with fun hobbies and sports. Start off with exposing them to interests that they may have, or flip through a sports and recreation center catalog for ideas. Magazine stands can also offer some ideas. Feel free to Google the top 50 crafts and hobbies for some ideas. You can also check with local parks, libraries or your child's school.

Some examples could be:

Tennis	Soccer	ping pong
Bike riding	painting	model building
Swimming	hiking	kayaking

You can also plant a garden together or create an emergency food pantry or a natural disaster shelter. You and your child will both get a good work out with the garden, and your child will get a lot of valuable knowledge on how to store food. And you can be creative with what you want to plant in your garden, or store in your emergency pantry.

Tip 10 - Give them opportunities to socialize

I went out to a restaurant with my wife and two boys. My wife alerted me to look at the table beside us. It was a couple also with two boys. However the parents were viewing their cell phone applications. One boy was playing on an iPad and the other was playing his Nintendo DS. Nobody was socializing with one or another. They were all in their own little world within their electronic devices. So I wonder how they communicate with one another when they actually need to. Do they just text each other?

Basically this tells me where our culture, and society is going. We are wired. And we are becoming wired to the point in which we fail to talk to each other. We forget to care about each other's day. We fail to interact and truly care about that other person in our life.

I'm guilty of this mistake too by buying my older son his own system. I purchased it because he didn't have other kids in the neighborhood to socialize with. I thought he could avoid complete isolation from peers by playing on line, and that it would make up for it. But it wasn't the same, not like actually and physically hanging out. Only some of the games were played with friends, many others were first person games without the need to interact with another human being. I've regretted buying him one ever since, because it hasn't given him the opportunity to meet new people and interact with people in the community in the manner in which people should. Instead, as if his whole life revolved just around gaming, his interactions just included his friends from his xbox live buddy list or the game characters in his solo video game campaigns and missions. And this leads to my next point.

Games, and other electronic devices can be great isolators. Games especially can place us in isolation when playing on campaign mode. When you're playing in the form of a secluded experience, you shut out the world, get away from people, whether it's strangers or family. You block out the real world and all its concerns and embrace a world you can control, a virtual and compelling world that cinematically unfolds around you.

Because of this, Kids playing excessively are loosing out on opportunities to socialize with other people, to build social skills and to make new friends. By playing without any interaction with other people in a real environment, they are basically crippling their own development as a person and member of society. They are not engaged in real relationships and conversations, and may forgo opportunities to court future mates, or to develop healthy long lasting friendships that will shape their character. This isolating experience may also make them miss opportunities that may open up new opportunities in areas of their life that they may wish to pursue.

And if one thinks that a child is still gaining some kind of benefit from interacting with virtual characters that speak, then any benefit would be limited to say the least. The dialogue and social encounters they come across in the game with other characters is not a substitute for the real thing. It's artificial. When things go wrong, you can start over, or you can just waste them without real world consequences. And since we have so much control of the environment, we want to resort to limiting dialogue and just focus on dialogue that leads to a desired outcome or completion of the game. There is no real human like interaction. The conversations with the "in game" characters are just a temporary engagement to reach an objective.

A mindset remaining in that virtual world makes it difficult for that person who's been playing for a long period of time to readjust when introduced to social settings back in the real world and truly embrace a conversation and expand on it with the intent of social networking. And doing so is necessary, not just in school, but in the career world as well.

And another thing gaming might unintentionally foster is the desire to be a recluse. This is something I've observed in myself. It was as if nothing else could compete with the world I just left behind. The other person's basic attempt to speak to me became boring and less gratifying. And as they spoke, I fought distracting images of my virtual world playing in the background in my mind interrupting my attempt to be a good listener. I found myself wanting to just return to my game and my life of solitude. And you don't want your child preferring solitude instead of companionship, especially from an early age.

Dating may be also become affected if your child is too absorbed in video games. How can he or she grow into a man or woman and develop the skills that are needed to foster a healthy relationship with the opposite sex. How can your child learn to know intimacy and the wonderful things a relationship can bring if he or she can only think about how to solve problems in games or outperform his friend's in competitive play in his first person shooters?

Kids may assume that interacting with simulated characters of the opposite sex is like having relationships in real life. It's obviously not. Again the non-playable character has only so many forms of interactive dialogue. This perception can be a wake up call especially if rejection results in an actual encounter. Dating in real life, breaking up and real conversation, gives us the insight to embrace new relationships; learning what works and what doesn't, understanding that not everyone has the same interests, and that not everyone we meet is compatible over a long period of time. That includes friends and future mates.

So encourage your child to meet people. Encourage your child to surround him or herself with friends. Make new opportunities for your child to do this on their own. This may also help draw them away from excessive gaming.

CHAPTER FOUR

Why I stopped playing

I am a parent, a teacher and an educator of 20 years, and a former gamer who has played off and on since the 70's during the early days of Atari. In fact my gaming started in the early years of childhood when my sister and I first got our Atari system. It was the 1970's, I was 8 years old and I recall riding a bike with a friend at times to the nearby catalogue warehouse center known as Gold Key to inquire about new releases of games such as *Asteroids*. Other games on the system included *Pong, Circus Circus, Haunted Mansion, Space Invaders, Adventure*, and *Combat*. And these harmless games were fun.

Since the system had multiple ports, I would recall playing with my sister and my father on games like Outlaw and Combat. It was a simple system with blocky figures against a basic screen. Yet it was fun and entertaining. Even neighbors would come over and we would devote an hour or two to play a game like *Night Driver* after playing outdoors or swimming in our pool. Games at that time only consumed a small portion of our time. Maybe because of the basic graphics or design of these games, we would simply move onto other things.

Much later, into the early 80's, computers like the early Macintosh had come out with their version of video games. The Atari had received new competition like calico vision; but they didn't interest me as much. I had moved onto other things. And even the hand held's, popular as free time preferences in my eighth grade classroom were catching on. Yet they didn't seem to have much more than a simple bleep moving across a two-inch screen. For example, my game DR. Dunk was fun, though it still lacked the appeal that modern games of today have. The moving bleep on a screen just wasn't enough to keep me interested in pursuing those early versions of handhelds.

After leaving middle school and pursuing high school, games were in the background though I was now more interested in girls. In fact, I had met my first girl friend, and going to party's and hitting the social seen to me was more on my mind. I still played, but gaming was reduced to trips to the arcade in the Sherman Oaks galleria. Games like *Gauntlet, Joust,* and *Packman* were some of my favorites. The fighting games were fun too.

It was this time too, high school, when I began to develop an interest in the world and the condition of the planet. I was becoming a concerned environmentalist putting focus on the disappearing rainforests. I was joining organizations like the Sierra Club and Green Peace.

As my interests in the environment grew, I also developed an interest in writing and in art. I had taken a class at West Valley Occupational Center on weekends, and in my free time I would pen ideas down for stories whenever inspiration came. I would even read my younger sisters stories and found her style to be an inspiration for me to put my mind on harnessing my talents as opposed to gaming.

In my 12th year of high school, I decided to take an environmental science class at the local community college; not just out of a growing interest in it, but because I had also needed to offset a failing grade in a geology course. I was very interested in the class and how it focused on pollution and ecology while urging us to a growing call to arms in protecting this fragile planet.

After high school, in the year1989, I went on to join the California Conservation Corp., an organization funded by the state government that served to protect and manage our natural resources and that was created during The Great Depression. It was one of the best times of my life. I was outdoors working on environmental projects in the Del Norte Center of Northern California in the Pacific North West, a place everyone called God's country. Exhilarating to say the least, I was building fish dams in streams and planting trees in forests out there instead of just reading about other people doing it in a National Geographic Magazine. My dormitory, an abandoned air force base, had a beach for a front yard and a forest for a backyard. The only gaming that took place was the occasional Macintosh game in their community Library and nights of D*&D with friends. It was awesome.

On occasion, when I would come home for visits from the C.C.C., I would play on the early Sega system; games like *Sonic* or *Shining in the Darkness*. In fact these games were probably the first to keep me playing for more than a couple of hours. I had completed the second game and had put it on the list of all time favorites because of the plot twist and colorful images.

I remember that I was so hooked in that particular game that while playing at night in the garage I nearly jumped 10 feet when my cousin came in to check on me.

A year into the C.C.C. program, I decided to get involved with their exchange program. I applied to work in Australia with a dozen others and was chosen. It was 1990, and I was traveling up and down Aussie land in a bus with the ATCV. There I had met other Americans from the states who had the same interest in traveling and taking care of the planet. I was enjoying my time so much and didn't realize I had cut myself off from the media back home. I had been on long camping trips, and hardly missing the movies or new games that were coming out.

It wasn't until I got back home in 1991 that the breaks seemed to come on. I had been living an intense life an now returned back home to find I was cut off from friends. Some of my closest friends had joined the armed forces and were away from home, others had simply drifted away or had gone away to college.

It's at this time that my mother, working in an office at school, pointed me in the direction of the Los Angeles Unified School District. So I applied and began working in schools and in special education classrooms as an assistant. It was fun. Yet I still went home board since I had lost contact with friends and looked for ways to fill my free time. I enrolled back into community college not sure about what I wanted to pursue; deciding between Environmental Science or Creative writing. So I took classes in both as well as general education courses.

Not long after enrolling in community college, I walked into a *31 Flavors* and found myself reacquainted with a friend.

She was able to get me in touch with a group of friends that I had often played the sport of paint ball with in high school. I had hit the jackpot.

Upon calling them, it was like I was one of the guys again. They were into everything, living life to the fullest. Paint ball resumed, movies, and *Star Craft* (the beginning of what would soon become an addiction). It was *Star Craft* that made me realize the potential of taking gaming to new levels; playing in groups and enjoying the trash talk. The idea of everyone in a room with their computers hooked up playing a game they could each interact in greatly appealed to me.

At this time, I had also wanted to buy a new car. So I decided to look for a second job in the evenings. A coworker, I met at one school, had been working at a place called New Horizons; a place that helped adults with mental disabilities. I took the second job, and It's there that I met my wife. I had dated her for some time under a vale of secrecy and protest by her family due to their cultural beliefs that Armenians should marry only Armenians.

I had still stayed in touch with my reacquainted friends, and with another close friend who had returned from the army. He in turn introduced me to a new friend who was also into gaming, comics, and movies. And I introduced them to my *StarCraft* gaming buddies from high school enlarging our gaming community.

So now I was busy, juggling life between dating, hanging with friends, work and college. My circle of friends continued to game, play paintball and do exciting new things. We would even go to board game conventions and my first E3, the famous

Electronic Entertainment Expo in Los Angeles. One particular friend in my gaming group had even introduced me to miniature games (which would later prove to be another vice) while on the way to play a paintball game in Palmdale Desert. So my love for gaming, miniatures and miniature dioramas had begun.

My wife and I continued dating then married in 1995. We had managed apartments in West Hollywood, living in one of the units in order to get a place and move out of my parent's house. After 2 years of marriage, and in 1997, we had our first son. I was enrolled in a community college moving at a snails pace wondering about what major I should pursue yet taking classes part time while still working as a paraprofessional and assisting a teacher and students in schools within the Los Angeles Unified School District.

It was within my first year of marriage that I got a job at the good guys and got my PlayStation 1. I was playing games like *Tomb Raider* and the *Legacy of Cain* for at least 2 – 3 hours a day. In fact when my first son was born, I would resume playing as soon as I got back from visiting them in the hospital; while his mom was probably propped up swollen in her hospital bed I would return and play my games.

When my wife returned home and resumed her routine I would then leave her the television to go to my computer and try to chisel away at my screenplays, novels, or play games on the computer like solitaire or games like *Balder's Gate*.

Eventually we moved out of the apartment and back into the San Fernando Valley. We managed a larger building, a 65-unit apartment building, in Van Nuys, and I was happy to be back into the valley and close again to my friends.

So in addition to my day job and night classes, I was required to be more involved in the management process. I would spend time in the leasing office often checking the grounds for problems. It was a nice building and provided me a room that I used as an office. There I had my bookcase, my toy collection with Fantasy figures and statues resembling characters in the games I would play. And I had my new Gateway computer, where I would continue to write my stories and play *StarCraft* in the free moments that I had; sometimes playing for hours over the Internet.

It was around this time our fights really began to escalate. In fact, one particular fight was so bad that I had lost my group of high school friends, the friends that I played most of my games with, when my wife involved them in one particular fight. In anger, I decided to take a trip to Cancun with the intention of having an affair after hearing from a Tai friend that there were brothels there. I was determined to even the score, and so I went with revenge and confusion about whether to continue or end the marriage.

When I returned, my anger cooled, and my wife convinced me to stay. It was a big mistake looking back, yet I decided to. Some friends I would see frequently, my friend from the army, the comic book friend he introduced me to; and occasionally my Tai friend and a friend I reacquainted myself with from my CCC travels in Australia. The other friends from high school, my *StarCraft* crowd, were now gone making no effort to reconnect with me as a result of our conflict. Never the less I continued with the marriage and the conflict in my marriage continued, and gaming seemed to be a venue to escape it.

After the completion of several games on my PlayStation system, I decided to give it up. I realized I had been playing to long and began to feel eyestrain, and an altering of my vision to some degree. I was seeing too many floaters, and my eyes would become dry. And so, with the advantage of being a school employee, I had sold the bundle (Some games weren't even open yet.) to a student at a school I worked in for a fair price.

As the pressures of managing the 65-unit apartment increased on both of us, we decided to stop managing altogether. Through an acquaintance of my wife, we were able to find a room for rent in a large home in Woodland Hills. By doing this, we had relieved some of the stress in our lives. Especially since I was now at CSUN working toward getting my bachelors degree so that I could teach, and she was pursuing her real estate license.

After what seemed to be a short abeyance of gaming, I would soon return to it. I would say that it even evolved. When my nephew's father gave my first son and I an Xbox the degree in which I played began to define me as a gamer and not just someone who played video games. *Halo* was the game of choice, and the halo parties that would last into the morning hours had started. And even though my homework at the university became harder, I still found time to play. In fact I was so hooked on gaming that I found myself playing on 3 platforms; my Xbox, my Nintendo DS, and my computer. I was now a video game Junky, an addict regardless of the controversy over its application toward someone who plays games too much.

It was 2005 and we had decided to move and buy a house. It was just before the housing crisis, and I was also closer to graduating from college. At this time too, I had upgraded to the Xbox 360 and my older son was now a seasoned gamer, playing games not appropriate for his age but at the time didn't seem to matter.

My second son was now born, and I found myself watching him as my wife began to show homes. And so I played on between diaper changes; letting him rest beside me while I played *Elder Scrolls*. His mother was out working longer and longer hours trying to sell houses, so often, that I was left watching the kids and feeling like a single parent. I was also now a recent graduate and teaching a classroom as a substitute teacher, teaching in regular classrooms and Special Ed classrooms.

At this point our marriage was at its breaking point. We were behind on payments and it appeared that we were going to loose the house. Stress was off the charts and it seemed that infidelity was a way to cope. And although I used much of my income and some of my school money on trying to save the home, it had been in vain. We lost the home.

From that point we had no choice but to move into a second property that my parents had acquired. The move had displaced my sister and her kids, but put a roof over our heads. She and her two kids had moved back into my parent's home.

While living there, we had told ourselves that it would be temporary. We also realized that there was an irreconcilable rift between us, in addition to the recent passing of my father, more stress related to my new profession, and the debt we had put ourselves in. Things had become so bad between us that I had even used one of the rooms in the 3-bedroom house, not only as my office, but also as a mini apartment. I lived in there, with a day bed behind me. It was also my man cave. I had my flat screen and entertainment center now purchased with my teaching income, my painting table where I assembled and painted my miniatures, my bookshelves stocked with fantasy books, and my day bed. The only things missing were a refrigerator and a bathroom. I had now started to completely isolate myself from not just her but my sons too.

My affairs continued until one night. While procrastinating on beginning a homework assignment and playing *Gears of War*, I received a visit from my wife and younger son who had entered my domain. She had a complaint with a list of things to fix in our new place, and we had argued. Being angry and with stress levels that had taken me to a breaking point, and having consumed some beer, I decided to leave and have another affair. And though I was in flight, I began getting this intuition that it was not a good idea. I feared that I would get aids, or that I would go to hell. I pressed on with a mixture of anger and anxiety brewing inside me.

I returned, not listening to that warning voice. And soon found myself with the likes of paranoia (loosing it). The paranoia began to increase. Then much of what I described in this preface began to unfold. I had begun being tormented from within.

As much as I hate to say this, I would have preferred the disease then separation from God, even though many will say its all delusional. This thing Christians call spiritual warfare is something I could have never contemplated; and the research I've done has only sickened me. I so had hoped that it was just some kind of nervous breakdown, but as I have done more research on it, I'm finding that it is something that is interfering with our lives in ways we can hardly imagine.

At this time, I am not gaming nearly as much as I once had. I may play an hour here, two hours there, but not 8 to 11 hours a day. I am separated for various reasons. And I am fighting to realign myself with my life's purpose and to fight two wars on two fronts; the spiritual one, and the environmental one. Both are very grim.

CHAPTER FIVE

Gaming was keeping me immature

Sadly my mind had been completely conformed to "THE GAMING AND MOVIE" world. Like Calvin in "Calvin and Hobbs" my imagination would run wild. While stepping into a dressing room at Macys, I thought about a zombie attack and how the area was not a good place to run to or defend from. There was no escape route. Other times I would jump through the opening of a closing door just in the nick of time as if I were Indiana Jones.

I even envisioned scenarios of games I played when I wasn't even playing. I started to become infatuated with elements of games like *Fallout 3* which had me thinking more and more of Armageddon and a possible nuclear apocalypse. It even inspired me to become a "Doomsday Prepper" and research bomb shelters and food pantries (which in the end may be a good thing, provided I don't take it to the extreme).

I often pictured people building underground shelters. I thought more and more about global warming, a possible viral outbreak, or the collision of an asteroid hitting Earth. A sense of fear and obsession began to take me in which I started focusing on 2012. I thought much about a world in desolation, possible death from a giant solar flare hitting the earth, or an invasion from an enemy nation, but not much about a spiritual after life, or a positive change in my life that would lead to real inner peace and harmony. I now sadly realize that's dangerous. It's almost as if the devil wants people preoccupied and distracted in an unprepared and worried state of fear instead of a prepared state of concern and action. And that's what I was; unable to hear God's voice, (or that little voice inside of us).

Not that zombies could have attacked at that moment I was at Macys, or that I was bored trying on shirts my wife picked out for me; it was just that I was constantly entertaining that immature side of me that shouldn't be going on when your back in the "Real World". Not for a grown man, anyway. And if it's not video games then it's Hollywood that fills our heads with such fantasy notions. And that's where the problem is, I was missing out on the stuff that matures us; things like retirement, financial security, my marriage.

And I'm not saying that everyone does that. Though I'm sure there is a good majority of people who do and may think about the craziest things, especially when stuck in traffic. And I think our media has a big influence redirecting our concerns. I was disconnected from life when I engaged in fantasy. I ran from my stress. So in ways I sometimes found my self -fabricating silly and unrealistic solutions to life's problems; unable to sift through the silly notions in order to find a workable one.

A game like Star Wars has people obsessed with its' creation, spending an unhealthy amount of their time on Earth obsessed about it instead of dealing with more important things; just look at all the people who relish it in its various forms. They dress up like the characters, they collect the toys, recall famous lines and mimic the actors, and they fantasize about such worlds being a reality, hoping that somewhere in the cosmos of space is another planet with life like those in Star Wars with an acceptance of just letting this one slip into oblivion. And on Halloween, many of us (and I've witnessed this) spend more on our costumes than we do on the kids, wanting to go out as if to rekindle our youth or avoid departing from that part of our self centered past that we should have grown out of.

In my experience of what I am going through, I found that I suddenly had a self-realization of what I had become. It was like a flash before my eyes. I found that what I surrounded myself with were toys, games, and movies. I was like a big kid that never grew up. My mind was partly shaped by what I had put into it all theses years. And that's why I found myself more immature for my age than say someone my age fifty years ago; or with other people who are just more responsible and mature. My father, my neighbors, people older than me, they all seemed more mature. They seemed to have their priorities right (their ducks in a row, their stuff together, their head on strait). They didn't come off as immature in conversations. They didn't hide behind toys and games. They could have an intelligent conversation about their careers, about their family life, about the real world and political concerns.

Maybe because of my interests, I often found myself gravitating toward teenagers when my wife and I would go to family functions. That was mainly because I had none of the same interests as the men or people we would see. I knew more about the Nintendo DS, about games and movies, much of what it seemed peers my age new little about. (Although gaming has become a growing trend) And so I often found myself talking to my wife's teen-age cousin instead of his father or her other relatives.

Maybe, like television has been accused of, video gaming can also shape the minds of young children into growing up to become immature people by forming unrealistic expectations that distort reality early in life; maybe by increasing the alpha wave activity in their brains, or maybe by the content they're exposed to. We need to remember, however, and make sure kids remember, that video games, and movies are an artificial world, and that which is learned from games may not be applicable in the real world.

Now that I've stopped gaming, I've gained a new perspective of my life and of myself. It almost seems like the last 20 years have caught up with me. I'm a man not a guy or boy anymore. I'm more focused on world events and how laws made in Washington and in our state government affect me, as well as how outer events unfolding will sooner or later impact my life. All those years of excessive gaming have robbed me of growing up.

CHAPTER SIX

Gaming was a big Enticing time waster

Now looking back I can easily say that I have played enough over the past 15 years of my life to equate it to just a little over two years of my life. That's basically spending two years of my life in cyber space. If you think about it, 10 hours a week adds up to 40 hours a month to 480 hours a year. I was probably playing 15 hours during the week, and another 15 hours on the weekend. That adds up to 30 hours a week, 120 hours a month, 1,440 hours a year. After 15 years it adds up to 21,600 hours. Sadly some gamers play more than 50 hours a week, especially if they're playing role-playing games. They are nearly living their lives in their gaming universe.

Some time back, while watching a show called *Aqua Teens* on a channel called Adult Swim, there had been an announcement. It was November 25, 2011after 9:30 pm to be precise, and the University of Louisville's head football coach had blamed his team's 21-14 loss to a rival team on the release of Modern Warfare 3. Which sounds crazy until we tell you it's not." The announcement went on to say that, "*Skyrim* and *Modern Warfare* will ruin your life and our ratings. Use that controller and we both walk out of here losers."

Later a commercial for *World of Warcraft* came on with Chuck Noris approving the game as the commercial professed that there are Ten million people in the *World of Warcraft* game. These two incidents occurring on the same day on the same station basically indicate to me that we are becoming a nation of gamers, maybe even a world of gamers that are less focused on the issues that we all need to play a bigger role in.

I totally praised gaming in the past. I used to think it was an art form. Now I know it to be more of a distraction to both kids and adults. It is a distraction from family, from your goals and dreams, your problems and relationships. And seeing this now is like stepping out of the matrix and seeing everyone else wired in while who knows what is going on around them. And you want to yell, Snap out of it! Get unwired!!!

I often wonder what I would be doing if this strange experience didn't happen. I guess instead of writing this book I would be looking forward to my next game and spending countless hours playing. I would still be living the party teenager high school life in a grown man's body without taking care to really plan for a quite possibly dim future, without creating a food pantry and learning how to grow my own vegetables and put my real concerns to the forefront.

And you might say that your not addicted, that you just love playing. That's fine. I agree games are awesome. But at some point though, when you begin playing for hours, what you're really saying without realizing it is that you prefer your simulated reality instead of your real reality. After all if your real life was great; in a loving relationship, great career, good health and a network of hobbies and friends, would you still be playing as much?

I'm not alone in believing that games can be addicting. I want to include this little incident. I was recently prompted to comment and review the game plant vs. zombies. Checking on other People's responses, I saw how many claimed it to be great and addicting. One mentioned it was a great way to kill some time. And after giving it a try, I found that it's pretty hard to just play one game. Don't forget the restart after you fail the level is like starting another game. Sometimes I would restart up to five times before clearing a level. The total was a cost of an hour, and I just wanted to relax and play for a few minutes.

I guess it's ok to game when you have to waste time, but you should not consider completing a game as if it is a serious priority in your life. It's not. Your kids are. Your bills are. God is. Your family is. Your career, your education is. The planet is.

And so my conclusion about Gaming is meant to be a hobby or pastime to be enjoyed in moderation. Its like, "OK, I played a while. Now I'm going to mow the lawn." Its not meant to be a device to make us entranced addicts. And that's what I'm beginning to see out there...not just our country but also now all over the world.

PART TWO –

ADVICE FOR THE ADULT GAMER

I'm going to be straight out. Gaming shouldn't be your highest priority. You should be working on your life's purpose and your highest potential. And if you don't know what it is…ask your self and ask to be guided to it. Chances are you'll know.

The reason I say this is because you will be in your twenties, then your thirties, and before you know it your forties. And gaming conceals this process from you. In fact I liked gaming so much that I told friends I gamed with that they would find me with a controller in my hands when I pass away in my eighties. I had no intention of giving it up or pursuing things that, now looking back on, matter more.

So here are some questions I thought of that might help you reflect on your situation and help you find more meaning in your life.

Ask your self these 3 questions

Why am I playing so much? Am I avoiding something that needs to be addressed or trying to escape from something? If so what is it and how can I fix it? Whatever the problem is, gaming won't resolve it; because the problem will mostly likely still be there when you've stopped playing.

What is my life's purpose or what is it that I really want to do with my life instead of playing 8 hours a day? If you know, make it your top priority pursuing it and devote more hours of your day to it. Also focus on the things in your life that you want to improve on, whether it's your financial situation, your health or your relationships.

What needs to be improved in the lives of my kids, my spouse or other close members in my life, and how can I improve it? If it's their financial situation, their education, or health again gaming for hours won't fix it. So take action, read with your children, look into money saving strategies, and join a gym with the significant others in your life. Regardless of how you aid them in their situation, deal with the problem first, and then return to your game.

CHAPTER SEVEN

How Gaming played a negative role in my marriage

When I found myself not happy in my marriage, I would escape from the real world. I found comfort in my character in the game *Fallout 3*. He was better than me in real life. At least I, my character, was fixing things and helping people in a ruined world rebuild it. It was simulated though. However, in real life I was ignoring my family and cheating on my wife, while ignoring the inner part of me that was crying out for change to either fix or leave my relationship.

I made little time to evaluate my life and consider a plan. And Since the first day of my marriage my whole life until most recently had been about playing video games. Often times to escape the stress of marriage or life.

Purchasing games caused arguments over money management. I constantly had to justify why I was buying the game. Sometimes I even had to hide it and sneak it into my collection. I would leave it in my car only to retrieve it later. It's a problem if you're supposed to be buying groceries with that money.

Some arguments also occurred because at the time we started out with only one television. So if I played more than enough hours she would miss her shows. And vice versa. I was missing out on game time, if she was watching her shows. I would try to get in my gaming time, especially when friends wanted to play, and be upset that she was on it.

Games also interfered with my dream of becoming a writer; it took up valuable time in my time slots that may have lead to a success as a writer if I had been writing in those hours. It blocked attempts to increase our household income by distracting me from networking and making a greater effort in writing or pursuing scripts that could have gone to publication or to a screenwriting contest. My gaming time could have been used for an increased course load in community college that would have accelerated the pace of me becoming a teacher and improving our financial situation and moving into a house that was supposed to be our collective goal.

Later into our marriage, after having children, some arguments occurred as a result of playing games that contained negative content with the kids. It didn't occur to me at the time that playing Halo with my 8-year son would be a bad idea. The rating of M didn't register, and I justified our shared game time as a bonding experience.

My younger son got into trouble at school after we had played the *Pirates of the Caribbean* game. We would get calls from school that he was swashbuckling at school instead of doing his schoolwork. Again the game rating indicated it was not age appropriate for him.

Now I see how I could have spent time with family instead of neglecting my marriage and children. Had I not put so much time into my games, who knows, I may have written some Sci Fi novels. After all it was once a passion and my dream. I'm also sure my relationships with my spouse could have had fewer arguments had I done more around the house, or put more effort into my attempt to secure additional income to pay down bills.

Sadly the warning signs were there. My son's mom had even made a comment years ago in the beginning of my marriage to my parents who were visiting that I spend more time with *Laura Croft* (the female character in the video game *Tomb Raider*) than I do with her. That should have been my warning sign to deeply consider our relationship and our channels of communication.

Now I find myself broken, separated and internally a mess. I see myself not only separated from my wife and kids, but from what I could have become. I live my life now wishing I hadn't had this awful alteration. And so I write this book, hoping to redirect you onto better paths.

CHAPTER EIGHT

Advice for the married gamer and non-gaming spouse

It's to my understanding that games are now another contributing factor to marital distress and break down. A friend I recall actually left her husband as a result of it. She remarked that all he did was play games, and she had to take it all upon herself to keep their household in order.

It was frustrating for her to have to work a second job to make sure that the rent was being paid. In her eyes I'm sure she felt like she wasn't a wife but a baby sitter for a teenager who should have been on the same page... working toward making the marriage work and improving their financial situation.

Another woman complained about how she felt ignored when her husband played games for hours in his man cave above the garage. She felt that the room, his man cave, he played in, was a definite contributor to their domestic problems. These are just two examples, (a third example if mine is considered). I'm sure it's a problem across the country by now, maybe even across the globe.

Women you can help your man stay away from gaming or game less by initiating marital discussions and seeking counseling. I found that being controlling or confrontational about it only made it worse. It basically pushes your spouse further into his man cave.

Draw him out of his man cave by giving him credit every once and a while when you don't see him playing. Make an agreement that you'll let him game for a few hours without ridicule or guilt trips if he follows some of the items on the tip sheet below or addresses some of the requests that you have that would improve your relationship.

Monitor him (or your child) and don't let him seek his game as an escape. If he's not happy and spends too much time in his man cave, make an effort to repair any damage early on (Don't wait and let it escalate) that was caused by resentment or anger from past or recent arguments that resulted from gaming. Remember, men can't read your minds. You have to tell us.

Find out what shared interests you both have and actively engage them. For example if you both like gardening or doing home improvement projects, set up a time for addressing those projects and try to stay committed to it. Setting a schedule or a routine for those things keeps it in your spouse's mind so that he or she doesn't game during those times.

Make regular nights out with friends like going out to shoot pool or play a board game. Weekend outings are good especially if you can leave the kids (if you have them) with someone. And even go out to explore new restaurants. Finding new favorite restaurants among the many you visit can be a new hobby.

Beware of the man cave itself. (Women might have them too). Find out if it's not really just a cheap alternative to getting a separate apartment. If your spouse is in it all the time then it's just like being single while being married. And if that's a problem have a discussion about it and try to find a compromise. Overall it was a bad idea for me because I began to isolate myself in it. And that seemed to help split the family up. And it's a really bad sign if your spouse is sleeping in it. Those are warning signs that should be addressed.

And guys, I suggest not encouraging your married non-gaming friends to start playing, especially a long online RPG. I recommended Guild Wars to a friend, and all though he had been gaming on his Xbox 360, he was not used to an online RPG game. In fact I recall him saying, "You are like a crack dealer. My wife really thanks you." In other words he was hooked on the same game I had been spending too much time on.

Finally, Below I've included some tips that could help ease the tension when you (the gaming spouse) play. Hopefully this information will help your marriage move from conflict over gaming toward a more harmonious and positive direction.

Tip 1 - Clean the house before you play.

Don't let your spouse see you playing in a filthy home, especially if he or she is coming home after a long day at work. Women, and I'm sure men, like to see a clean home. It's one less disappointment they have to be concerned about. And a clean home is a happy home; it raises the energy through out the house.

And if your not Mr. Clean or Marry Poppins, then just do the best you can. If possible see if you can make a contribution toward hiring a house cleaner to come twice a week, then just do your best to keep it from getting dirty again.

Sometimes just a quick pick up can do the trick. Simply pick up kids' toys, mop and sweep, vacuum and clean any counter tops.

Tip 2 - Cook dinner.

Another nice thing besides keeping the house clean is cooking a meal or having the evening meal ready. It doesn't have to be special, but if your spouse sees the contribution they're liable to be thankful for it.

And it is ok if you're not Chef Ramsay or Anthony Bourdain. Places like Costco have already prepared dishes like lasagna that you can just place in the oven then serve. They also have prepackaged salads and other quick items. Before you know it you'll become creative and come up with all kinds of creations.

You can also pick up a cookbook or "YouTube" a recipe if you decide to whip something up yourself instead of going with something premade.

Tip 3 - Bring your spouse a gift.

A gift can be anything from a music CD to flowers. It lets your spouse know that gaming isn't the only thing on your mind. It reminds them that you care and that he or she is important to you.

Some examples of gifts for a wife or girlfriend could be as follows:

Her favorite perfume   A favorite movie DVD
Jewelry   A gift card
An article of clothing   A good book

Some examples for a boyfriend or husband might include....

Sports tickets   Cologne   Clothes
Sports equipment   Electronics   Tools

If your spouse is the main player in the home I would strongly advise getting something other than a game so that you don't feel in anyway that you have contributed to more playing. In fact a gift that would take your partner away from the game like movie tickets or concert tickets might be a good idea.

Other gifts that might be something that could bring you together as a couple might include:

A board game
Tennis rackets or sports gear
A group gym membership
A Karaoke machine
A trip or a cruise

I'm also sure that as your relationship progresses you'll discover other things and interests that your partner likes. My advice would be to look for those things as you continue to learn about your partner, and take turns nurturing those interests in each other. Find a common interest that will pull you both away for a time.

Buying stuff for the home also counts. It could be groceries, or a new appliance for the home, or some new furnishing for the home. And Guys (gamers) don't feel bad about it, especially if you're buying food with your "hard earned" money instead of a game. Food's a necessity. What would you rather have if a Big Earth Quake hits, a stockpile of food, or a stockpile of games?

Tip 4 - Give your spouse a foot or back massage.

It takes that stress and tension out of them, and the massage could lead to something special (sex incase your wondering;).

If you can't give your partner even a simple 15-minute massage then get them a gift certificate to a spa. Although the advantages of a personal massage from you, is that it could lead to intimacy, some healthy conversation and quality time.

To learn how to give a simple massage at home, I would refer to a couple of "YouTube" videos or a book on the subject. Or go to a Spa with your spouse to get an idea. Just remember that like anything else you get better with practice. So by the fifth massage you should have it right.

TIP 5 - Watch a movie together

No excuses here. Both of you need to spend that quality time together. So get a baby sitter or leave the kids with your parents, and go see that movie. And even if it's not your kind of movie see it anyway. It's time well spent, and if it's a "Chick-flick" it's 3 hours at the most. And you (speaking to guys) might actually enjoy it.

Also encourage your spouse to compromise. Make One week a Chick Flick, the next a Guy Flick. Or see a movie you both want to see. Staying home and watching a movie that's been rented works too. You're still spending quality time together taking care of your relationship.

If you have kids, see family movies. You can also have a family night where you break out the popcorn and watch a good movie.

TIP 6 - Watch the kids

If you have kids, give your spouse a little break. Watch them so that he or she could go out for a bit. Give your spouse some cash too. This will really score some points.

You might be thinking, well what am I going to do with the kids for two hours? Here is a list for the frustrated gamer that isn't used to spending time with the kids:

Take them out to see a movie, the mall, or a friend's house.
You can take them to the beach
You can take out a board game
Play a sport with them or build a model together
Take them out to the Library
Take them to the park, or a local carnival
Read a book with them

If the child is a toddler or a baby, then do diaper duty and have them just play with their toys on a blanket in front of you. I also recommend taking a parenting class and a child

CPR class to reassure your partner that everything will be all right.

As a last resort you can play a video game that allows for multiple players. Wii is great for this. You and your kids who should be old enough to play can have a great time with this. Just keep the games E rated.

Finally there is a second concern I want to add to this section when I say, "Watch the kids." **Watch the Kids!** If your both gamers make sure the kids are being cared for and are always properly supervised. A story surfaced in the past about a Korean couple. Apparently they were too busy gaming that they neglected their child, leaving the child to starve to death. Similar reports have surfaced elsewhere. The show called "The Guild" even has a mother who is a *World of Warcraft* addict that finds strange ways to occupy her kids so that she can game.

TIP 7 - Join an organization or club together

You can volunteer your time together making the world a better place and helping your relationship grow. You can both find something you love and enrich your lives. I have a list of some organizations in the next segment, and you could look online for more.

A club, like a hiking club or tennis club could also be a good way to spend time together and meet new people.

You'll also be getting your exercise in and the opportunity to travel. There are all kinds of clubs out there and many that will lead you into new interests. Meeting up with other couples too can give you new insights.

CHAPTER NINE

Get involved

Many of you, I'm sure, play for hours. I know that I used to, especially games like Fallout 3, *Skyrim* or *Guild Wars*.

In the game you're making the virtual world a better place… You're rescuing the princess…the hostages…the kingdom. You beat a game complete all the levels.

However, "The real world", the one you return to after the game, is still there. After those hours of play you accomplished something in the game but not in the real world. No positive changes have been made in the world around you. What have you done to make the world you return to a better place? What have you done to affect those around you in a positive way? In those hours, have you developed mentally, physically, or spiritually? Have you performed any good deeds? Have you become a more responsible person, contributed to society? Have you earned a raise? Have you improved your life or solved your real problems in the real world? My answer is that it probably hasn't.

The world needs our help! So get involved. Join an organization or charity today and give back. There are organizations and charities out there that work toward solving the many problems that are out there. And they need your financial support. Many of their websites also allow you to volunteer your time.

Volunteering may also help you develop new skills or lead you to make a career change. In addition to this, volunteering looks great on a resume.

The following is a list of organizations that you can get involved with and a brief description about what they're about.

ORG.

Description

Heifer International
P.O. Box 8058
Little Rock, AR
72203-8058
(800) 422-0755

World Organization that helps
3rd world countries out by
giving them livestock

GreenPeace
702 H Street,
NW Suite 300
Washington, DC 20001
Greenpeace.org
(202)462-1177

Environmental Organization
with a strong emphasis on
protecting the Arctic ice and
Oceans

World Wildlife Fund
1250 Twenty-Fourth Street, NW
Washington, DC 20037
Worldwildlife.org
1 (800) 960-0993

Environmental Organization
dedicated to protecting
endangered species

Wounded Warrior Project
4899 Belfort Road

An organization that helps
returning veterans who

Suite 300
Jacksonville, Florida 32256
Woundedwarriorproject.org

are suffering from high
rates of suicide and trauma

St. Jude Children's Research
    Hospital
501 St. Jude Place
Memphis, TN 38105
1-800-231-3441
stjude.org

An organization that
helps children fight
cancer

International Fellowship
of Christians and Jews
30 North LaSalle Street, Suite 4300
Chicago, IL 60602
info@ifcj.org
800 486-8844

An organization that
helps Jews who are
in need and are
being persecuted

Heal the Bay
1444 9th Street
Santa Monica, CA 90401
www.healthebay.org

An organization that
monitors the Santa
Monica Bay and
California coast

Paralyzed Veterans of America
7 Mill Brook Road
Wilton, NH 03086
www. SupportVeterans.org
1-800-555-9140

An organization that
helps disabled
veterans find
medical treatment
and support

International Campaign for Tibet
1825 Jefferson Place, NW
Washington, DC 20036
www.savetibet.org

An organization that
helps people in Tibet
maintain traditions
against Chinese Oppression

Union Rescue Mission 545 S. San Pedro Street Los Angeles, CA 90013 213 347-6300 www.urm.org	An organization that helps feed the poor
Defenders of Wildlife 1130 17ᵗʰ Street, NW Washington, DC 20036 www.defenders.org/join 1-800-385-9712	An organization that helps protect wildlife throughout America.
Union of Concerned Scientists Two Brattle Square Suite 6 Cambridge, MA 02138 www.ucsusa.org	Another Organization concerned about Global warming and the serious state of this planet
National Wildlife Federation Operations Center P.O.Box 1691 Merrifield, VA 22116 1-800-822-9919 www.nwf.org	An organization that works to preserve the habitats of wildlife
Save The Redwoods League 114 Sansome St. Suite 1200 San Francisco, CA 94104 (415) 362 – 2352 SaveTheRedwoods.org	An organization working to preserve the redwoods and forests of the Pacific North West

American Civil Liberties Union
125 Broad Street
18th Floor
New York, NY 10004
www.ACLU.ORG

Works to preserve our
rights and our freedom

Hope of the Valley rescue mission
8165 San Fernando Rd.
Sun Valley,
CA 91352

Works toward helping
the homeless in the
San Fernando Valley

Marvin Gross
Union Station Homeless Services
825 E. Orange Grove Blvd.
Pasadena, CA 91104
(626) 240-4559
www.unionstationhs.org

An organization that
helps the homeless

National Parks Conservation
   Association
777 6th Street, NW, Suite 700
Washington, DC 20001
npca.org

An organization that
helps protect our
State Parks

FINCA
1101 14TH Street, NW, 11th Floor
Washington, DC 20005
FINCA.org
(202) 682 – 1535

An organization that
helps poor people
around the world
by giving them loans
with your donations

World Vision
P.O. Box 70359
Tacoma, WA 98481

Gives loans and gifts
in the form of farm
animals or supplies

Worldvisiongifts.org
1-888-511-6511

to people in 3rd
world countries

The Nature Conservancy
4245 N. Fairfax Drive,
Suite 100
Arlington, Virginia 22203
(800) 628 - 6860
Nature.org

An organization that
protects threatened
land by buying it

Doctors Without Borders
PO Box 5023
Hagerstown, MD 21741
www.doctorswithoutborders.org/
   concact
(212) 763-5779
(212)679-6800 donar serv

Supports doctors
that volunteer to
help people

Friends of the Earth
1100 15th Street, NW
11TH Floor, Washington, DC 20005
1-866-217-8499
foe.org

An environmental
organization that
heal the planet

Sierra Club
85 Second Street, Second Floor
San Francisco, CA 94105
www.SierraClub.org

An organization that
fights against
corporations that
pollute the planet

NRDC
40 West 20th Street,
New York, NY 10011
www.nrdc.org

Protects Natural
Resources

The Wilderness Society
1615 M Street, NW,
Washington, DC 20036
Wilderness.org

Protects wilderness
and wildlife

Planned Parenthood
434 West 33rd Street
New York, NY 10001
www.plannedparenthood.org/
    member

Helps families
overcome the
problems of
early parenting

SPCALA
Los Angeles Society for the
    Prevention
of Cruelty to Animals
5026 W. Jefferson Blvd.
Los Angeles, CA 90016
1-888-SPCA-LA1
www.spcaLA.com

Helps protect
abandoned dogs,
cats and other
animals.

Attn: Director/President
Conservational International
2011 Crystal Drive, Suite 500
Arlington, VA 22202

An organization that
that protects the
jungles across the
equator.

ASPCA.ORG
888 773 2221

An organization that
rescues animals

Amnesty International
amnesty.org
1 Easton St.
London
WC1XODW, UK

An organization that
helps protect human
rights across the
world

Aidswalk **AIDS Walk Los Angeles**, Los Angeles, CA. 11751	An organization that helps find a cure for Aids.
Battered woman's shelter Downtown 442 South San Pedro St Los Angeles, CA 90013 Phone number (213) 680-0600	Helps woman escaping abusive relationships
The National Center for Missing and Exploited children Charles B. Wang International Children's Building 699 Prince Street Alexandria, Virginia 22314 USA Missingkids.com	Helps find missing people

CHAPTER TEN

Don't go to Hell

Now if you're married, it was probably in a church, Temple, or some other place in which a religious ceremony took place (unless it was a justice of the peace) to wed each other. My advice, especially after what I experienced and mentioned in this book's preface, is to get your butt to church and don't drift away from your belief system; and maintain a healthy relationship of worship and a healthy marriage.

It's often easy to forget about God and our purpose here on this Earth when life's demands overwhelm us. And it's also easy to forget when we're having too much fun playing.

Spiritual Warfare

Believe me when I say that the enemy of our souls (The darkness, the forces of entropy, the fear and darkness instead of the light at the end of the tunnel) is out there and has such things as stress, sins of iniquity, unfortunate circumstances, the world, the flesh, and spirits to assist in leading people away. And if you also listen to George Noory and Jeff Rense, and probably everybody at your local church, you'll hear about people with a similar story. Just YouTube stories about the afterlife and dark entities like shadow people. You'll find tons of stuff and too many people suffering from it, and some of these people aren't even affiliated with religious beliefs or cults. And other people, who can confirm this bizarre stuff, don't even want to talk about it because it's too scary and strange.

Like me, they were just going about their life and it just fell into their lap. And it can't be delusional if too many people are coming into agreement with what they're seeing, and their descriptions hardly deviate.

There are even television shows in which ghost hunters go looking for this, wanting to catch a ghost on film. You might say their findings are just unexplained phenomena, magnetic anomalies, energy fields or hallucinations. Well these things are real and do mess with your mind and brain much like a computer virus messes with your computer. And shows out there and segments on YouTube, and reality television shows that research haunting and Ghosts, only sadly seem to validate this as my jaw drops confirming my suspicions.

This subject is disgusting to say the least. It's like adding one more problem we have to be vigilant about, one that's behind the scenes, behind the veil. And sadly encounters with these entities seem to be becoming more prolific everywhere.

So if you're all ready in the middle of this, on meds thinking you've lost it; you're not crazy…and you're not alone. As I said the information about it is out there. Do your research.

Everyone needs to become aware of the issue and turn away from the stuff that feeds (this dark energy). Such activities or acts that invite lust, foster hate and other negative human emotions are self-destructive in the long run and should be decreased. Throwing your child's demonic looking statues and toys away (listed above) is another thing you can do to correct the problem.

If you starve this dark energy out by turning away from what feeds it, (like turning from sin), prayer and meditation, raising your vibrations (those positive vibrations) and begin doing things that are the opposites of old behaviors like acts of love and kindness instead of lust and selfishness, your energy begins to change back into a positive kind.

I also find keeping yourself busy, working out, being productive, and spending less time with your own company especially if your inner self is a bitter jerk, or you're in a constant hating mode, helps. You'll know more about what I'm referring to when you meet other people and you are feeling loathing toward them on the inside. Purge that bitterness and hate before it consumes you!

Drawing away from a Godly life

I can't say that gaming is strictly responsible for my drawing away from God. I did have a troubled marriage too that filled me with resentment and offense. However, I do know that in my attempt to escape from my unhappy marriage, I devoted my time to my games, and made it one of the main focuses of my life. I had pushed God, and everything that God represents, further and further into the background. I wasn't putting the household at the top of my priorities, I wasn't going to church; I wasn't praying, and most of all I wasn't taking an inward look at myself. It was as if I was a selfish teenager in party mode all of the time. I wasn't listening to that little voice (call it intuition) that's inside of us, always trying to guide us in the right direction.

I had my philosophies, but they didn't keep me in line with a moral righteous life. They definitely didn't get rid of all that pent up un-forgiveness and hate that built up over the years. In fact, it seemed as though my beliefs masked the problem and diverted me from becoming aware of my offenses and inward hate toward myself.

Gaming became idolatry, a vice to indulge in continuously hours without end. In fact, playing video games found its way to the top of my priority list where as the more important things were left off of it or pushed back.

Now looking back, about few years ago, before this religious ordeal and event, I had a different list of priorities. I was reading fantasy books and had a large collection of books on my shelf. Some of those books were based on fantasy characters; *Lord of the Rings*, and books like the *Dragon Lance Series* or the *Dark Elf Trilogy*. Next were my miniatures. I had many of those too. I had planned to paint them and assemble battle scene dioramas with demons and Orcs battling elves and dwarves. And if I wasn't gaming, reading fantasy books, or painting miniatures, I was pursuing some other vice, like pornography that was also unhealthy to my growth.

And all of it was dark and definitely didn't resonate with goodness and light and maturity.

I was forgetting about my family, my neighbors and the community. I allowed my life to be absorbed by my gaming instead of coming out of my shell, my inner man cave, in order to fellowship with my community and do good things in the world. And although I pursued high goals like a college education, I neglected the pursuit of improving the quality of my inner life and in fostering a healthy soul, a healthy community, and a healthy planet.

My desire to write books, and what I believe to be my life's purpose and passion, was also on that priority list. However it was at the bottom of that list, and I didn't apply as much time as I would have liked in completing that goal. In fact I could say it was a god given talent that I didn't pursue with the free time that I had. And this is why I advise parents in the previous chapters of this book to direct their children's free time away from games and toward their talents.

Looking back, I think, maybe I should have been in church or prayer on Sundays, as many would say, and on family outings; spending time with the kids. I would do that now, but the damage is done. My life is nothing like it once was. It has fallen apart and I'm now just beginning to rebuild it. Life around me has become strange and bizarre as if I have returned to it like some disoriented actor returning to some new unfamiliar and twisted play.

And remember that, regardless to whether you are skeptic to my claims or not, any kind of distraction turns our attention away and basically helps let the bad guys (the negative entities) or corrupt people in power, win in the world and universe. Keeping us occupied with the weapons of mass distraction means that things go unchallenged. Then we become blindsided. Whether it's the break up of our family and marriage or something on a larger scale, we are taken from our duties and neglect to fight the good fight and stand up to Tyranny. Next thing you know you have a chemical waste plant in your back yard, or your rights that you took for granite are suddenly gone.

Pollution of the soul

Pollution of the soul surrounds us just about everywhere you look in the forms of Pornography, music with foul lyrics, and movies with more gore, violence, and perversion than they contained in the past. And now we're beginning to see it in games. Our cyber characters begin to pursue the negative things games offer such as, sex and nudity, tobacco and alcohol, guns and violence, magic and sorcery, and profanity; depending on the game you play whether it's *Grand Theft Auto, Gears of War* or *World of Warcraft*.

It seems that we live in a culture fostered by movies, television, music and games in which we are placed in a frame of mind where, "Devastation is cool", "Violence is cool", "Suicide is cool", "Sexual immorality is cool", "Demons are cool", and "Apocalyptic wastelands are cool". And this mentality and these associations seem to help separate us from things that are important to our development, and of a more clean and benevolent nature; things that are important to our salvation, and important to our moral character. The things **that bring us closer to God**, the overcoming of trials, the need to forgive and seek forgiveness, the need and search for true guidance appears to be lacking.

I call it all spiritual pollution because it contaminates us with images that often remain in our minds. These in turn become distractive thoughts when we have no need for them, like appearing in the background during a simple conversation with someone. Any of this pollution seems to feed the flesh in the sense that it becomes the wallpaper of our minds, shaping or influencing our thought processes that lead to our decisions, actions and hence outcomes. And the more we fill our minds with it, the more corrupted and filthier we become. Evidence of this often appears in our own vulgar conversations with our peers. It often was in mine. And again I am talking about this as being a problem when done in excess, not in less than moderate amounts.

Take pornography for example it can come in two forms, soft porn or hard core. The hard core is taking humanity to its depths. And some might say that moderation here is ok, but what's moderation? Would that be once a month, once a week or once a day? Do you control the amount, or does it control you?

A preacher once said during a mass I had attended in the past, "that you can't have both feet in the world, or one foot in the world and one foot in the church." He was basically saying that you can't serve two masters. Games beyond moderation push more of our relationship with God away. We spend less time with God. God gives us a life and time to fill it with our talents. And it is displeasing to see kids and adults consuming too much of their time with a video game instead of filling that time with things that are going to create a mature, loving and productive adult.

A Growing Sea of Filth

Now putting everything under the magnifying glass, I often wonder about humanity. The act of creating, caring for others, expanding our minds, is the ultimate pinnacle and should be the norm of our species. Yet we seem to be growing an attraction to crude sexual and filthy acts, and causing harm to others physically in the real world and vicariously in the virtual one. And the media and internet has made it possible to engage in these things at the push of a button or flip of switch, where as before it was taboo in some remote part of our civilization.

And I'm wondering, how can we be entertained by the garbage of our earthly experience, the lower aspects of ourselves over and over and over again.

And because the laws have changed, and society has taken a more liberal and tolerating view on things like pornography, movies with graphic content, and dark video games, we find ourselves surrounded in a sea of filth that just seems to become filthier and filthier and distancing us from the good things in ourselves, in the good aspects that humanity has to offer and from the architect of this universe.

Basically I am saying that the collective conscience, in the form of media, seems to be going in a dark or unclean direction. It almost seems like, in this country and now spreading to others, that we're being bread to believe that everything is hopeless in our lives and in the world, and that we need an excess of material things and the comforts of bad vices to cope with it.

This excess and devotion to this hedonistic attitude might even be a reason why the nation of Islam calls us the Great Satan, the land of hedonism. (Jihad vs. Mcworld). Not that

I agree with their perception of this country to that extent, nor obviously the tactics used to express their frustration, but they may be right in that we have walked away from our values and holding what should really be dear; God, Family, the community, and now which should have been addressed long ago (and what the Native Americans warned us about) the ecosystem in high esteem. Even soldiers coming back from overseas will tell you that kids overseas respect their parents, its almost the other way around over here.

It's my belief that while everyone is bickering about what God is and who's religiously correct, Satan and the Forces of Darkness are having a field day knowing that this world has the potential of becoming a living hell because of collectively creating an unhealthy planetary system that has become too overburdened, too polluted, and too exhausted. As a result of this, droughts from the new warmer conditions (because of less ice and less trees on the planet) will increase and so will food shortages. Then, sadly, wars will follow. In addition the worlds economies (manipulated by the globalist elites that have no interest in anyone's welfare but their own) will collapse, allowing them to push their agenda. Their goal is to bring all nations to ruin. And they will blame it on overpopulation as if to justify their massacre while hiding behind their lies; refusing to tell us that its not so much because of over population but because of poor management and policies like the Pacific Trade Agreement and other policies that they themselves engineer.

Spiritually damaging

According to the definition of Spiritually, (attaining growth in the areas of a person's inner life and physiological processes) playing games can lead one away from improving their quality **of life in pursuing a spiritual path.** It can corrupt them by depriving them of any kind of spiritual experience and it can fill the player (both child and adult) with an indulgence for content that may be violent or distasteful.

Basically excessive gaming is spiritually damaging because it appears to nurture an unhealthy spiritual attitude of putting oneself first. Playing games, collecting games, trying to focus our time on the nice plasma television sets and surround sound systems to enhance our **gaming experience pushes God and the prospects of a healthy mind and spiritual life** out of the picture and instead places our focus back on our selves.

When I played, it was ME, ME, ME, and the rest of the world can just disappear. And as I look around I see others doing the same. People run out of their homes to line up for the next big game launch then run back into their homes to loose themselves into oblivion for hours on end. And by doing so we, as excessive gamers, continue shifting our values, our time and priorities toward things **less important and at the cost of humanity's future and our sanity.**

And so we grow older and time marches on. And we become lovers of ourselves when all we are doing is spending our time engaging in things that entertain us, the things that stealthily grow darker and darker (and we become like the frog in boiling water). So when Christians say that in the end times men will be lovers of themselves, its because we are wrapped up in ourselves, our toys, instead of addressing the deteriorating condition of our future.

I continue to observe life unfold around me, but now with new eyes. I see that what complicates us now is not just the addictive pull gaming and other forms of media have on us as a society, but the growing level of darkness in it (and quite possibly harmful subliminal content inserted by malicious factions rumored to exist in the Industry), and we as a society are loading that data and media in our minds daily. For example, we might watch an hour of television and choose to watch a show like *True Blood* over a show like *Grey's Anatomy*. The difference in watching a show like *True Blood* over *Gray's Anatomy* is that *True Blood* is a dose of something dark, a vampire (basically a demon) feeding on humans. We are filling our minds with people drinking the blood of others in that hour, becoming used to it, desensitized to it, and maybe secretly identifying with it.

That "Dark" gaming content can tarnish the goodness in us simply because it is darkness and not of light or love or the qualities inherent in pursuing a spiritual path, with a clean, clear and mature mind. Often times this dark content is hidden in movies like *Mega Mind* by DreamWorks Animation (2010) that parents take their little kids to see. There is a particular scene where after defeating the good guy, Metro Man, Megamind brings out a radio and begins playing the song "Highway to Hell" by ACDC to celebrate his victory and his plans for a new world order.

Humming this to yourself is dangerous when you begin to understand the complexity of the subconscious mind. This is why it's so important to be consciously vigilant, and again why I stress that gaming isn't for kids. It certainly isn't without serious restrictions and enforcement.

And devotion to movies like this in addition to other things, like excessively violent games and pornography, is **competing with time with God** and things of a good spiritual nature that are filled with real life and light. Such things provide that healthy contrast against the dirtiness of this world. And if by now, at this stage in your life and after reading this far, you recoil at the mention of all of this, its possible that the energies I speak of have worked their way into your persona - hardening you, keeping you in your chicken coup or boiling pot.

And to be fair and after I have done more research, I understand that it's not all our fault that we surround ourselves with material things to comfort us. It seems that we have been programmed and conditioned to do so since our early childhood in the forms of advertisements and media campaigns. So when we seek comfort from stressful events in our lives we run to those things, turning them from hobbies to vices. We must be consumers and buy, buy, buy and indulge in the material world. It seems too often these days to be our temporary fix for our stress instead of going to prayer, engaging in a good workout, taking the time to meditate, read through scripture or have a moment of self reflection in the middle of some quiet time.

However, **I find that when we pursue the more Godly things,** we are kept in the right and in a place safe from dark influences. It's as if we are put back into alignment and reengage in the process of repairing the damage that was caused by unhealthy behavior. We are also in commune with others in a state of good will.

I want to add that even for those of you who are like I was, agnostic or atheist, and believe this section and parts similar are unnecessary because of the lack of proof, I just have one question, a question that formed after this occurred... "When you go to a funeral, where is it held?" And then I realized, like brushing my teeth, or making routine visits to the doctors, or taking my car in for maintenance, **it appears that church, love and ethical conduct are also an integral component in our busy lives.**

Many scientists are beginning to come to realize that there is a composer to this universe who made it and us. Scientists will also agree that everything is made up of energy. And in regards to God and Gaming, think of life as a SIMS game. You are the character in the game, and God the creator is the observer and player. Would you want to see all of your subjects or characters sitting on their couches doing nothing but watching porn or playing games all day? Or would you rather see them composing masterpieces and creating new technologies while making the world a better place with the talents they've been given? I would get pretty bored with the first scenario.

CHAPTER ELEVEN

The positive aspects of gaming

When it's in moderation, and I'm speaking in regards to gamers over the age of 15, Gaming is great. It's an interactive art form that pulls you into a different world with its own problems that you can actually solve. The imagery is amazing, the artwork is incredible, worlds are brilliant, and its' clear that an incredible amount of imagination goes into making games.

The stories are engaging and have evolved to the point that they've become more compelling especially in the Role Playing Games. And some games, if not many, are being written by best selling authors, including some that have inspired me.

In many games, especially the harder ones, challenges helped me to develop problem-solving skills. They helped me to become analytical in my approach to finding a solution.

More positive things to say about Gaming are that they gave me a sense of triumph after beating a boss or completing a difficult task. It's like the equivalent of watching your favorite team score a touchdown. You walk away amped and pumped up. Its like my inner hero is being adorned and nurtured. I'm sure in some way, deep down inside, it helped build my ego and self esteem too. Though if it did, I would have preferred the act or event to have happened in real life so that the glory could have been known.

Over the years all kinds of games have entertained me and made me laugh or have enchanted me. In coop modes they provided me an opportunity to have a great time with my friends at system link parties or online through Xbox live or its equivalent on the other systems. And to my satisfaction I have had many of these gamer nights that have started at night and have ended in the morning with empty pizza boxes and soda bottles littering the floor.

Games also gave me, a creative person, the ability to design and create within the game. Whether it's customizing my character, modifying weapons, or decorating the inside of a new home.

I felt relaxed (when I wasn't being attacked by wondering monsters) when exploring incredible landscapes. With ambient and classical styles of music playing in the background in games like *Marrowind*, and *Skyrim*, I would happily wander off in search of treasure or secret weapons as I explored fallen ancient ruins and hidden locations. Doing so seemed to relieve my tension and take my mind off of any problems that may have been troubling me that day.

These are only some of the reasons I played. However, even for all of my reasons, it still comes down to the fact that life is short. And it moves quicker as you get older. And all of those games... are just games. None are any different than any other. Their purpose is still to draw you in and entertain you.

CHAPTER TWELVE

Conclusion

Basically, my concern is that you're going to turn off your game system one day to find out that you've messed up your spiritual life, and that the problems of the world aren't at your doorstep, they're in your homes and have overtaken you.

These are definitely tough times and it seems like everything out there is trying to make us DARK or derail us. Things that come into our homes, that we think are harmless, may later prove to be otherwise. We might think we control our vices, only to find out later they seem to control us.

For those of you that believe in a life after this one, (and for those that don't even after what I've mentioned in my preface) it appears that the price of a better life, this one and for the next is constant vigilance. We need to continually be aware of what we bring into our lives, and into our homes.

And if it seems that I've repeated myself here or in other parts of this book, it's because I can't emphasize how important it is to follow the advice given. Excessive gaming has the potential to do so much harm in ways we can understand and in ways that we are only beginning to comprehend.

Again looking back, I see how it has stolen years from my life, interfered with my marriage and family, my personal growth and pursuit of my dreams, how its' made me immature and has desensitized me to things considered demonic.

So my parting words to you are: If your marriage is in trouble, your gaming isn't going to fix it. If your weight or socializing skills are an issue, gaming isn't going to fix it. If your kids are becoming more aggressive and their grades are falling, gaming isn't going to fix it.

In parting words I just want to add the following. Like Gandhi said, "Be the change you want to see in the world" So get involved, balance your time and priorities, and be vigilant of your actions. In doing so, you will begin to make the world a better place.

www.ingramcontent.com/pod-product-compliance
Lightning Source LLC
Chambersburg PA
CBHW050404290526
45786CB00003B/1115